Advance Praise for
WATERING THE RHUBARB

Charles Goodrich's poems celebrate the body of the earth from which we come and to which all things return, as well as the power of poetry to raise its fist—full of seeds, its only weapon—against oppression. These poems share the comfort of ravens, "black wings banked around the coals of their hearts,/their bright minds/ smoldering," the particular, fleeting tang of whortleberries, and the minerally kiss of cold water drawn from a well. Contemplating the uncomfortable, such as aging, the risk of tsunami, and the self-inflicted erosion of habitat and democracy, these poems nonetheless point our eyes toward the hawks, not the "hawkers of hate." This is poetry wholesome in the best sense, showing us how to preserve our wholeness and the flow of grateful energy amid the obstructions (major and minor) of our worldly lives.

— Karen Holmberg

In an age as coarsened as ours, we are startled by a voice so guileless, and a heart so open, as Charles Goodrich's. Read, and be restored.

— John Witte

In *Watering the Rhubarb*, Charles Goodrich combines his knack for humor and his lyrical voice to evoke empathy for a natural world we humans live in but often do not appreciate. He has a keen ear for using sounds to evoke emotion. There are many things here we will think about long after the book has been read and placed on a shelf.

— Barbara Drake

These poems vividly display a reverence for the beauty of the natural world and a deep lament for its endangered status, but what makes them most interesting to me is the signature wry humor of their creator and his unique contrarian spirit.

— Clemens Starck

WATERING THE RHUBARB

Flowstone Press

WATERING THE RHUBARB

Charles Goodrich

WATERING THE RHUBARB

Copyright © 2022 Charles Goodrich

All rights reserved.

Cover Image © Ian Boyden. Used with permission.

First Flowstone Press Edition • April 2022
ISBN 978-1-945824-52-4

Flowstone Press,
an imprint of Left Fork
www.leftforkbooks.com

rhubarb:
1. the edible, fleshy leafstalks of *R. rhabarbarum,* used in making pies, preserves, etc.
2. *Slang.* a quarrel or squabble, a heated dispute on the playing field.

> And I go outside and gather
> A handful of fresh vegetables.
> It isn't much to offer.
> But it is given in friendship.
>
> > Tu Fu, from "Visitors"
> > translated by Kenneth Rexroth

TABLE OF CONTENTS

I

Faith in Seeds	5
Shine	6
Winter Riches	7
Miracle Fatigue	8
Three Poems on Marys Peak	
1. Seismic Activity	9
2. Solastalgia	10
3. Closure	11
Birds Dying of Old Age	12
Earthworm's Credo	14
Summer Blood	15

II

Ravens, Ten Days after the Inauguration	19
At Neskowin on Presidents' Day	20
Camped beside the Metolius River in the Third Year of Trump's Presidency	22
The Former South Vietnamese Soldier, Recruited by the U.S. Army Airborne for Parachute Missions along the Ho Chi Minh Trail, Who Says He Felt Betrayed when the U.S. Abandoned His Country in 1975, Explains Why He Doesn't Hate Americans	23
Unclogging a Drain During the Impeachment Trial	24
A Tall, Stiff Drink	25

III

Breakfast at Waldo Lake	29
Springs in the Desert	30
First Love	32
Instead of an Elegy	33
Who Are You Rooting For?	34
Overgrazed Pastures on the Kings Valley Highway	36
A Good Night's Rest	37
The Falling Season	38
Willamette Springs Memory Care	39
Hardware Serenity	40
Notes	42
Acknowledgements	44
About the Author	46
About the Cover Artist	47

WATERING
THE
RHUBARB

I

Faith in Seeds

Up on the ladder
I'm cleaning the gutters,
pausing occasionally to admire
the flight of the samaras
as they helicopter down from the maple tree.

Each ripe seed
is a one-winged bird
fluttering to the ground,
or a tiny boat with a single oar, striking out
toward an uncertain shore.

I've read that willows are migrating north,
and mola mola—ocean sunfish—
usually confined to the tropics,
have been found swimming in Alaskan waters.
The permafrost itself
may soon turn to mud
and go slumping off into the sea.

This old tree
has unleashed a storm of seeds this autumn
as if lightening its limbs
for a difficult trip.

But we're going to tough it out
right here, the maple and me,
keep on squeezing out samaras
and poems
even if they just stutter and twirl
through the weak, late-afternoon sunlight,
rarely sailing far from the tree.

SHINE

After a month of rain, we're all
a little depressed, light-deprived
and mush-brained.

Except for that snaggle-toothed
old conifer that stands alone
beside Fairbanks Hall.

It's in fine fettle, flexing
its muscles in the wind, green hair
glistening with rain.

A squall from the west
is like having old friends knock at your door,
fiddle, banjo, and hooch in hand.

Lucky the creature for whom rain
is moonshine. There'll be a hot time
in the downpour tonight.

Winter Riches

Early autumn rains blustered in this week
and some friends are already grumbling.
The oncoming darkness looms before them
like a sentence. They're getting
pre-depressed.

It's true that Cascadia is famous
for long, dreary winters
but the odd person flourishes.
As quick as the rivers rise
steelheaders pour out before dawn
to cast their lines onto fish-haunted waters.

Mushroomers
armed with baskets and small knives
get all bug-eyed
scanning the duff under fir trees
for king boletes and golden chanterelles.

And someone with a taste
for gray solitude, for the drab music
of guttering rain
and a penchant for gathering
words and phrases onto a blank page
may feel flush.

Miracle Fatigue

When the blossoms of the winter camellia
glowing white as bone China cups
through the late-February afternoon gloom
don't give rise
to even a glimmer of delight

I figure I'm just tired
of getting my spirit teased
by every trivial outburst of beauty.

But later when I notice
drops of dew
suspended from the fence wire,
each bead reflecting another whole world
like a necklace of disembodied gods' eyes

and I don't shudder or gasp,
I realize I'm suffering
revelation overload.

Yeah, I know: any moment's
run-of-the-mill exquisiteness
will never come again,
but I just can't seem to absorb
any more amazement. I'm sick of epiphanies,
weary of wonders.

Dear world, grant me
a few more weeks of restorative boredom.
Your glories will not be diminished
by the absence of my attention.
Come spring, with luck,
I'll be porous again.

Three Poems on Marys Peak

1. Seismic Activity

Scientists determined the earthquake
was centered a hundred miles off the coast,
4.2 on the Richter Scale, too slight
to be felt on land.

But I was sitting in the meadow
on top of Marys Peak that day
watching several species of wasps, flies, and bees
patronizing a lily—like hard-drinking aliens
at an inter-galactic tavern—
and I felt *something*.

Whether it was that distant
submarine temblor, or a sudden disappearance
of self, or just the mountain shrugging its shoulders
in stoic indifference,
I couldn't say.

2. SOLASTALGIA

Only a few big wildfires
in Oregon this summer
though Africa and the Amazon are ablaze.
How much time remains
in the 'gasoline crack of history'
is hard to say.

Regardless, it's a peaceful late-summer day
on Marys Peak. Silvery blue butterflies
zigzag among bedraggled lupines
following chemical scents
to nectar. Their haphazard paths bring to mind
impermanence—even in peaceable times
nothing lasts. And now
as the planet begins to overheat,
flowers, butterflies, and humans
are all going down.

The butterflies have flown.
I kneel in the meadow
and comb through the grass
looking for an ant or a beetle, any animate
miracle, any unwitting
fellow-traveler. Thus far
I've always been able to find somebody.

How strange
to be joyful in this moment
while afraid and homesick at the same time,
already nostalgic for things
that aren't quite yet gone.

3. Closure

If any of the locals—
and I'm talking about the folks
whose people have been around
since the last ice age—

wanted to walk up Marys Peak
and cold-camp alone—
to sit, to watch, to dream,
asking Creator for a song—

I'd be okay with closing the road for a week—
or even permanently—
if somebody comes back
with a really good song.

Birds Dying of Old Age

1

The sparrow decided
eons ago
that when her time came

she'd just give up
fighting the fleas and ticks
and lie down in the duff

and close her eyes
and let the little people
eat her back to the Earth.

2

Just let me get back to Mexico
the turkey vulture is thinking

halfway across the Gulf
his shoulder socket grinding with pain.

Back to my favorite tree
with the cow bones scattered underneath

and the beautiful view
across the empty chaparral.

3

The storm petrel was travelling solo,
riding a northeasterly off Kamchatka
when her heart stopped.

She crumpled into a feathered clump
and the wind held her aloft for a moment
before dropping her into the North Pacific.

4

A male Anna's hummingbird
laps up a nightcap from our feeder
then returns to his favorite viburnum.

As darkness descends
he latches his claws around a familiar twig
and falls asleep and never wakes up.

The scarlet feathers of his gorget fade
but for years his desiccated body will remain
perched there on the branch.

Earthworm's Credo

(S)he believes
that insight is never separate
from appetite

that obstacles do not exist
for one who sees the universe
as lunch.

Humble practitioner
robed only in mucus
her/his aim is modest:

to leave the earth
richer than it was
before (s)he ate it.

Summer Blood

I've cored and sliced, then sautéed
summer
in the giant pot

and now chop
the flesh of tomatoes
into bloody chunks

a heathen priest practicing
vegetable sacrifice.

I turn the heat down low
and let the troubles I can't do anything about
simmer
all afternoon.

Outside, autumn clouds
thicken into rain. The sauce thickens
and the bubbles erupt
more slowly.

If floods come, if friends
sicken or die, if another war erupts

there will be quart jars
full of the blood of summer

to feed and console
whoever may come
to open the dark cupboard.

II

Ravens, Ten Days after the Inauguration

—at Breitenbush Hot Springs

I came here for a respite
from marches and protests,
but all the naked strangers in the hot tubs
who usually want to talk about
their yoga injuries and cleansing diets
this evening are clamoring about
fear and politics.

So I hole up alone
in a ramshackle cabin
then wander at sunset through the old cedar forest
until five ravens swoop in so close
I can feel their wing-thrusts in my own chest
and taste their acrid cries in my throat.

Ravens, I realize. That's what I came for.
And when I awaken deep in the night
I think of the birds asleep on their roost
their black wings banked
around the coals of their hearts,
their bright minds
smoldering.

At dawn the ravens swoop back,
their harsh voices haranguing
whoever still sleeps.
Black wings flaring with sunrise, they drive
the night back into hiding,
and I head for home,
somewhat revived.

At Neskowin on Presidents' Day

Dingy green carpet,
pink Formica countertops, fragrance
of mildew and sanitizer—
I've always liked this motel.
And what better place

than a tsunami-doomed beach town
at the westernmost edge of the continent
on a faux national holiday
a month into this bogus administration's
avalanche of lies
to contemplate the erosion of democracy?

Pulling on my rain bibs and parka
I slouch out into the mist, nod to the guy
in the scuffed, yellow hard-hat
bucking up a big Sitka spruce
that blew over in last night's gale.

Out on the beach
amid the storm-wrack
a party of gulls eviscerates a dead seal,
pulling out the pink and blue entrails
like pundits dissecting
a gut-wrenching election.

With the drizzle thickening to rain
I trundle on, wondering
what on Earth can be done?
Vote. March. Send money. Undo the years
of gerrymandering. Write poems.
Spit in the ocean.

At the water's edge, a tall, shaggy man
is shooting video of his young daughter.
In blue fleece, pink tights and yellow boots,
she splashes into the shallows,
dragging a three-foot-long bull kelp
toward the waves.

No one can say
where our country is headed.
The little girl doesn't know
how it works. But I'm going to adopt
her brave, innocent attitude.
"Dad," she yells, "I'm putting it back!"
And she flings the slippery plant
into the surf.

CAMPED BESIDE THE METOLIUS RIVER IN THE THIRD YEAR OF TRUMP'S PRESIDENCY

How do you grow old living with failure and disgrace?
Stay close to the cascading creek: cold, shimmering.
—Wang An-shih

Late November. Shimmering stars
and a promise of frost. While the House moves
toward impeaching the President,
I huddle close to a little campfire, reading poems
composed a thousand years ago
by Wang An-shih.

A celebrated writer,
Wang was also a public servant
who rose to become Prime Minister.
He persuaded the Emperor
to build granaries, hospitals, and orphanages
and to lower the peasants' taxes,
a poetry-writing populist
of the Sung dynasty.

But Wang's reforms were anathema
to the government's well-heeled bureaucrats.
Sacked and banished,
he spent his forced retirement wandering forests,
visiting monks, meditating,
and writing these poems.

While nations and empires rise and fall,
mountains and rivers endure,
the old Chinese poems insist.
But the charlatans in the White House
want to mine the whole Earth,
and all I do is sit by a river
and write poetry.

The Former South Vietnamese Soldier, Recruited by the U.S. Army Airborne for Parachute Missions along the Ho Chi Minh Trail, Who Says He Felt Betrayed when the U.S. Abandoned His Country in 1975, Explains Why He Doesn't Hate Americans

First, he says through our interpreter,
we are Buddhists. We are taught from birth
to not hold onto resentments.

Second, we are young. Seventy percent
of our people have been born
since the end of the war.

And third, unlike the U.S., we are
an old country. We have been here
for a long, long time.

The American War lasted
less than two decades. The French
occupied us for more than a century.

The Chinese
have threatened our borders
for thousands of years.

We loom large
in the mind of your nation,
but you don't seem so big in ours.

Unclogging a Drain
During the Impeachment Trial

Toilet's plugged
and the bathroom sink drain is sluggish.
I was in the dumps already
over national politics.

Abuse of power.
Obstruction of justice.
I'm guessing the septic tank
is overdue for pumping. And meanwhile
we still haven't seen his taxes.

But even though I'm glum and angry
I can still do minor plumbing.
I run the drain-snake, work the plunger,
get the commode running.

Next, with an arm's-length of wire
with a little hook bent into the end,
I fish a wet, gray gob of hair-gunk
from the sink's P-trap
then pour baking soda,
salt, and vinegar down the drain
and wait for the chemical reaction to begin.

Even if the Senate trial
turns out to be a sham,
I love the sound when the blockage dissolves
and the sink drain hisses and foams.

A Tall, Stiff Drink

Some of our friends say
our well water tastes like nails.
Sharp with magnesium and iron,
it tarnishes our sink
and stains our clothes.

But on a sorry summer afternoon
when the so-called President
is demonizing immigrants, women,
formerly-loyal aides

I like to fill a tall glass with tapwater
hard and cold from deep in the Earth
and guzzle it all in one long tilt
before heading back out to the garden
to water the rhubarb.

III

Breakfast at Waldo Lake

Before the others are awake
I slip from the tent and go down to the point
to pick grouse whortleberries, the smallest
of the huckleberries, so sweet and tart.

Calm waves whisper along the shore.
Smoke from last night's campfire clings to my shirt.
Hovering in the south, Diamond Peak, still mantled
in late summer with dusty snow.

It takes half an hour to fill a tin cup.
I'll sprinkle a few berries on each pancake
and the children will gobble them up
still half-asleep, hardly noticing
how other-worldly they taste.

—Vaccinum scoparium

Springs in the Desert

—late August, Summer Lake Wildlife Refuge

Artesian springs arise here, impounded
and submerged beneath earthen-dammed
Ana Reservoir—a small, weed-choked,
holy body of water
close beside the high desert—
where I drift

mid-day in a little boat
trying to match in patience
the great blue heron skulking
motionless in the reeds
and the two old codgers
slouching in sling chairs on the dike
their fishing rods as still as the air.

A stooping northern harrier
makes the family of coots cluck and
lurch away from the shore
and a yellow-rumped warbler
darts from its juniper perch
to snatch a fly.

But that's it
for drama here
until a little red car
parks at the boat launch
and three young women
in bikinis and flip-flops
flap their beach towels onto the dock,
unpack a cloth bag, knapsack and basket,

and begin to cultivate
the afternoon.

Now as I float
at the edge of earshot,
the one with pigtails
reads aloud from a book, a novel
I'm guessing by the cadence of her voice,
while the dark-haired woman strums softly
on a ukulele, and the third one,
lying on her belly, a sketchbook
splayed in front of her, intently draws
with colored markers.

I won't paddle any closer.
I know better, after six greedy decades,
than to train binoculars
on the Muses.

I only wish I could tell them—
Thank you! Thank you for reading
and painting and making your music
at the edge of this desert.

I hear you. The starved air,
the dry brush, the dusty playa,
even those old fishermen
whether they know it or not,

and even the drowned springs
of the Ana River
all hear you.

First Love

Gratitude to my old
inadequate bladder
for waking me in the night.

Otherwise I wouldn't have been
pressured outside
to water the frost

and wouldn't have seen
beside the crescent moon
low in the east

Venus
shivering there
first love of the year.

—January 1, 2019

Instead of an Elegy

I'm composing an elegy for the dog
when a house-fly bounces off my nose
and settles onto the computer screen.

Aroused,
I lean in close to study her—
hairy legs with suckered feet, cellophane wings,
intricate red eyes, and a keen
pinpoint awareness.

Ever so slowly
I place my wrist against the glass
just in front of her,
take a deep, steadying breath
and snatch her up
bare-handed.

Still sad
but now also briefly elated,
I walk out onto the porch, open my fist,
and set the astonished fly free.

I know the dog
would be proud of me.

Who Are You Rooting For?

With baseball season suspended
I've switched to rooting
for nature, watching live-feeds

of chicks hatching
in an incubator in Kansas,
beavers building a dam in Alaska.

Donning my Mariners cap
I wander outside to cheer on
chickadees pilfering seeds from the feeder,

then walk the street, feeling the rush
of maple trees leafing out, the manic grace
of gray squirrels racing along power lines.

I can hear some of you virtual fans screaming,
"Hey, coronavirus is nature, too,
you bum!" And it's true. Diseases

are natural. Droughts, forest fires,
hurricanes, floods—made worse
by burning carbon—are still natural.

Death itself—natural.
So keep your distance
from the peanut vendors,

coughers, deniers, and hawkers
of hate until this strange, dangerous
season blows over.

Baseball will resume, and the Mariners
will mostly lose, but nature is never
not at bat.

Overgrazed Pastures
on the Kings Valley Highway

Forest fires to the north
east and south. The taste of smoke
permeates the car.

Heat waves warp
the dusty horses
and swayback barns.

A sudden updraft of vultures.
There must be an abundance
of death around here.

In the sun-scorched pastures
patches of Queen Anne's Lace
like elegies for snow.

A Good Night's Rest

All night nuts
drop from the black walnut tree
and plop to the street

and a car now and then
runs over one
with a resounding *crrrunk-POP!*

I crack the window above our bed
and listen in the dark.
What else will I miss when I'm dead?

Crows in the morning
picking the meat.

The Falling Season

We hate cleaning the gutters
before all the leaves come down.
At our age
the roof eaves loom higher by the year.

This fall the maple leaves
have hung on
well into November, and as of yesterday
the Japanese pagoda tree still had a full head
of golden foliage.

For weeks we've *oooh*'d over
the sweet gums in the cemetery,
squinted into
the gilded ranks of cottonwoods beside the river,
and watched the neighborhood oaks turn red
as my long-dead father's
raddled old nose.

But this morning
it's 25 degrees outside. Frost flowers bloom
on the dining room windows.
Chickadees flit from magnolia to feeder
more manic than ever.

Eating breakfast, we watch the dead leaves
rain down, knowing the time
has arrived. Let us toast
the falling season
with a new bottle of ibuprofen
and this afternoon we'll hoist the ladders.

Willamette Springs Memory Care

They've thrown up a new nursing home
on this brown-field site
halfway to Philomath.

Bland, rambling ranch-style,
must be seventy rooms
with a covered drive-through entry
like a motel.

There used to be a wrecking yard here
twenty years ago. Junk cars packed together
like patients in a ward, leaking oil
into the earth.
I found an alternator
for my old Ford pickup there once.

Window boxes dripping petunias.
Automatic glass entry doors
that glide open when they see you.
Sign says: Accepting New Residents!

I've vowed
never to let myself be put away
in such a place, although, of course,
I may forget.

Hardware Serenity

You wouldn't call sorting nails
meditation, exactly,
just a tedious, manual task—

tossing vinyl-coated sinkers into an old Bugler tin,
six-penny finish nails
into a plastic yogurt container. But I find it
oddly peaceful.

Early autumn. Mariners game
on the radio. Light rain
on the metal roof. Sixty-five
years old. Time
to get organized.

Roofing nails, ring-shank nails.
Staples and brads. Order
and decay. I'll put off sorting the screws
for another day.

Notes

page 10, "Solastalgia." The phrase "the gasoline crack of history" is by Williams S. Burroughs.

page 11, "Closure." The "locals" are of course the indigenous inhabitants of the Willamette Valley and coastal Oregon—whose contemporary members belong to the Kalapuya, Wusi'n and Yaqo'n tribes—for whom Marys Peak, or T'cha teemanwi, is a culturally and spiritually significant landform.

page 19, "Ravens...." In September, 2020 the Lionshead Fire burned half of the buildings at Breitenbush Hot Springs. The Breitenbush Community remains viable and is rebuilding a number of structures.

page 22, "Camped beside the Metolius...." The lines by Wang An-shih are from the translation by David Hinton in *The Late Poems of Wang An-shih*.

Acknowledgements

Thanks to the editors of the following journals in which these poems, sometimes in different forms, first appeared:

Catamaran
    Faith in Seeds
    Birds Dying of Old Age
    Summer Blood
    At Neskowin on President's Day
    Seismic Activity on Marys Peak

NewVerseNews
    Unclogging a Drain During the Impeachment Trial

Sediments, Sequences, and Solitudes (PLAYA anthology)
    Springs in the Desert

Tangram Press (broadside)
    Hardware Serenity

Terrain.org
    Miracle Fatigue

Windfall: Poetry of Place
    Willamette Springs Memory Care
    Breakfast at Waldo Lake
    A Long, Stiff Drink
    Camped beside the Metolius...
    Shine
    Overgrazed Pastures on the Kings Valley Highway
    Solastalgia

A video of the author reading "Who Are You Rooting For?" appeared in the Spring Creek Project's series "The Nature of Isolation."

"Three Poems on Marys Peak" was included in *ARTscend*, a collection of writings dedicated to Marys Peak.

Everlasting gratitude to my writing group partners, Rick Borsten and Gregg Kleiner, and my long-time co-conspirator, Clem Starck, for their astute feedback on many of these poems.

About the Author

Following a long career as a professional gardener and a decade as director for the Spring Creek Project for Ideas, Nature, and the Written Word at Oregon State University, Charles now writes and gardens at his home near the confluence of the Marys and Willamette Rivers in Corvallis, Oregon, within the traditional lands of the Ampinefu band of the Kalapuya tribe. He's the author of three previous books of poetry, *A Scripture of Crows*; *Going to Seed: Dispatches from the Garden*; and *Insects of South Corvallis*, and a collection of essays, *The Practice of Home*, and has co-edited two anthologies, *Forest Under Story: Creative Inquiry in an Old-Growth Forest* and *In the Blast Zone: Catastrophe and Renewal on Mount St. Helens*. His poems and essays have appeared in *Orion*, *High Country News*, *The Sun* and many other journals and anthologies.

More information at **charlesgoodrich.com**

About the Cover Artist

Ian Boyden—artist, writer, translator, and curator—investigates relationships between the self and the environment, in particular how art and writing can shape our ecology. The cover image is from his series of paintings, "Echoes of Earth."

More information at **ianboyden.com**

www.ingramcontent.com/pod-product-compliance
Lightning Source LLC
Chambersburg PA
CBHW052126110526
44592CB00013B/1762